A Christian's Musing

By

Elaine Jordan

Truth
Publications

Taking His hand,
Helping each other home. ™

ISBN 10: 1-58427-340-2

ISBN 13: 978-1584273400

First Printing: 2011

Truth Publications, Inc.
CEI Bookstore
220 S. Marion St., Athens, AL 35611
855-492-6657
sales@truthpublications.com
www.truthbooks.com

Table of Contents

Faith

The Giants Among Us

There are giants among us! These giants are those huge problems and worries that plague us. We worry about problems, such as the global situations, personal finances, and gang and drug problems in our schools. We are helpless to solve this endless list of gigantic problems. Some problems are close and personal, some problems affect our community, and all of us are affected by global problems. What can one person do? These giants are so big and so strong! They can overcome the most able person.

Faith in God helps us to face our giants. God has promised to always be with us and only requires that we follow His commandments. Since the age of the patriarchs when God spoke to Moses and Abraham, God has promised to be with us. God promised Moses that He would never leave or forsake him and the Israelites. As part of His promise, God parted the Red Sea so the Israelites could cross on dry land and led them as a pillar of fire at night and a column of clouds during the day.

As the Israelites prepared to enter the land of Canaan, God commanded them to send in twelve men to spy out the Promised Land. When the spies came back, ten of them were afraid of the giants inhabiting the land which were descendants of the giant, Anak. Only two spies, Joshua and Caleb were certain the giants could be conquered with God's help. The Israelites listened to the ten scared spies and did not depend on God. They let the GIANTS defeat them without any battle, because they only considered their personal abilities and did not count on God's help (Numbers 13:1-14:10).

After forty years of wilderness wandering, the Israelites again prepared to enter Canaan. Those same giants lived there! Moses tells the Israelites, *"Be strong and of good courage, do not fear nor be afraid of them; for the LORD your God, He is the One who goes with you. He will not leave you nor forsake you" (Deuteronomy 31:6).* This time the Israelites depend on God. Israel battled giants as they entered the land of Canaan. Og was the giant king of Bashan and was so big that he slept in an iron bed that was thirteen feet long! (Deuteronomy 3:11). All of Bashan was conquered which included the region east of the Sea of Galilee and extended south of the River Yarmuk into Gilead. So much for those giants! After defeating the Bashans, the city of Jericho was taken by marching around the city blowing on horns, not with a siege or battering rams or soldiers.

Even those giant descendents of Anak are defeated by Caleb, one of the two faithful spies. Both Joshua and Caleb were old by the time the Israelites are conquering Canaan and some descendents of Anak still lived in Hebron. Caleb asked for that portion of Canaan to be given to him to conquer! Caleb wasn't afraid of the giants as a young man and he certainly wasn't afraid of the giants as an old man. Caleb depended on God and knew that God was with him. Caleb drove out all remaining giants (descendents of Anak) and went on to conquer all the remaining territory north of Hebron. Caleb and the Israelites defeated all the Canaanite giants because of their faith in God. They remembered what Joshua had told the Israelites about God's commandments for conquering the land *"Have I not commanded you? Be strong and of good courage; do not be afraid, nor be dismayed, for the LORD your God is with you wherever you* go" *(Joshua 1:9).* Caleb knew that by depending on God defeating the giants was possible and demonstrated his faith by his leadership.

All of us know the story of David and the giant, Goliath. The Israelites and the Philistines had been battling for some time and the armies were camped on the hills across from each other in the Valley of Elah. The Philistines had the upper hand over King Saul and taunted the Israelite army with Goliath. Neither King Saul or any of the king's soldiers would battle the giant – they were afraid. David, a shepherd boy, told Saul, *"The LORD, who delivered me from the paw of the lion and from the paw of the bear, He will deliver me from the hand of this Philistine."* With a sling and five smooth stones, the shepherd boy killed the mighty giant Goliath. This story demonstrates that a battle with a giant does not require soldiers and swords, but victory depends on God. David slew his giant, because he had faith in God. In Psalm 18, David writes *"I will love You, O LORD, my strength. The LORD is my rock and my fortress and my deliverer; My God, my strength, in whom I will trust; My shield and the horn of my salvation, my stronghold. I will call upon the LORD, who is worthy to be praised; So shall I be saved from my enemies."* David truly leaned on God as he dealt with the giants throughout his life.

When we are battling our giants, we must remember to stand like Caleb and David. They stood with God and so they were not standing alone. In Matthew 28:20, we have Jesus' promise: *"I am with you always, even to the end of the age."* Standing with God, makes an insurmountable army to any giant!

Visiting Ephesus

I have a son in the Navy who recently had a short visit at Ephesus. He and some of his friends were able to walk the streets and amphitheaters of this Biblical city. My son told me how awed he was to walk in Paul's footsteps and how he could hear the angry cries of the silversmiths in the amphitheater. Just walking in the dust on the street and seeing the city made his heart swell with pride for Paul and Paul's companions. My son's respect for the early Christians grew phenomenally that day and he appreciated their personal faith and courage to teach others about the gospel.

The Biblical event that my son is remembering is the story in Acts 19 when a silversmith named Demetrius with the other silversmiths became an angry mob. The silversmiths were enraged, because people were not buying their silver statues of Diana anymore. The Ephesians had been taught by Paul and other disciples about the one true God and that silver statues were not gods. Of course this meant less income for the silversmiths and their anger was directed at Paul. The story climaxes with all the silversmiths, town officials, and some of Paul's companions in a theater. The silversmiths are mad and loud and wanted their livelihoods improved! The only reason the mob didn't turn deadly is one city official reminded the silversmiths that Rome would require an accounting for the day's "uproar."

When you read Acts 19 about Demetrius and the Ephesian silversmiths, do you feel their anger and have empathy for the silversmiths' situation? After all, the silversmiths must sell the silver statues of the goddess Diana in order to feed their families. This mob of silversmiths could have very easily turned into a riot demanding the end of all gospel teaching in Ephesus. The tension in the theater was thick and the Christians caught by this mob were in a lot of danger. Any catalyst meant a violent death for them. Can you smell the fear and sweat of these men? Do you appreciate their courage as they faced the theater full of silversmiths who wanted to blame their financial woes on them? Yes, the story in Acts 19 is about real people and real events!

When we read our Bibles, we should appreciate that the stories are about real people and are in the Bible for our edification and learning. The sights and smells and noise and songs of the Bible stories should be alive to us today as we read and learn about our Biblical ancestors. We know that those people ate and drank, were happy and sad, tired and scared, loved and hated. Biblical people lived their lives very similarly to how we live our lives today. Some lived in the dust of the desert, some in simple villages, and some in the big city. They had families and friends, lived through political uncertainties, paid taxes, and enjoyed God's creation. Bible characters were real people living real lives with the same concerns as we have today. The reason for including the story in the Bible is to help us to learn about God and to know more about the gospel.

All of us will not be lucky enough to walk in Ephesus where Paul and the silversmiths argued over silver statues. However, that is not the point. The point is that Paul and the silversmiths did argue and we know about it through our Bibles. These Bible stories are not just stories – they are real people living through real events. Learn from these stories and build your faith and courage as a modern-day Christian! Walk the streets of Ephesus with Paul as you read your Bible.

God is Alive!

How many have sung that wonderful hymn* where the chorus rings, *"There is a God, He is alive. In Him we live and we survive. From dust our God created man, He is our God, the great I AM"?* At my congregation, voices sing out loud and strong for this hymn. We love to sing about our God that is so big, His name is I AM. I have heard people say this song is a Christian's anthem, but do we walk the talk from the song? Do we live like we know that God is alive?

As of 2005, approximately 88 percent of the world's population were said to "believe in God" which is down from 96 percent in 2000. In the United States, 95 percent of the population "believe in God" (Cambridge University). There are 2.1 billion "Christians" in a world population of 6.7 billion — so almost one third of the world population believe in Yahweh, the Christian god. I am sure that all these "Christians" also believe in gravity. As part of their belief, they see the effects of gravity and depend on gravity. They don't do anything special to stay stuck to the earth, because of their belief in gravity.

The difference in being one of the 2.1 billion "Christians" throughout the world and being a New Testament Christian is following the guidance provided by God. In Matthew 7:21, Jesus says, *"Not everyone who says to Me, 'Lord, Lord,' shall enter the kingdom of heaven, but he who does the will of My Father in heaven."* A Christian must do the will of God to demonstrate his faith in God, not just believe in God. Faith is more than belief and adds effort and activity to a Christian's belief in God. Christians cannot know what God wants from osmosis or doing what feels right to them. Even new drivers study the handbook and practice for their driver's test in order to know what is expected of them and to learn the laws of the road. They cannot get behind the wheel of a car and hit the interstate without effort beforehand. They are required to know what is expected of them as part of being a driver. It is funny how a person understands that effort is required for driving, but does not expect to make an effort to know and understand God's will.

Since the beginning of time, God has told man what he wanted them to do. He walked with Adam and Eve in the garden, He spoke to the patriarchs, He gave the Jewish nation the old law and prophets, and He speaks to us through the Bible. It takes effort from the Christian to study and learn what God has told us in the Bible, but this is how we know God's will. When we know that our God is alive and is the great I AM, then we understand that we must follow His direction. Believing in God and knowing He is real are two different things. Conviction of our knowledge of God compels us to do the things that God wants us to do and requires effort to study and understand His will.

Then when we sing *"There is a God, He is alive,"* we know that we really believe what we are singing. We know that our faith in God is evident to others, because our lives put action to our faith. We work to understand God's will by studying His Bible and doing the things that God wants from us. Real belief in God requires effort from us which should be our pleasure; because we know that our God is alive!

---

*Song titled "Our God, He Is Alive" by A. W. Dicus

The Providence of God

The providence of God is the constant and wise foresight and care which God provides for His creation. God has provided for His people since the beginning of time and continues to provide for us today. Our omnipotent God made intricate preparation and plans for His creation and His people. Any person can see the complex synergy of our earth and the interconnections of living and non-living things. God planned how each part of His creation would exist and interrelate with the rest of His creation. The complexity of God's creation is not a Darwinian accident, but God's plan.

God made man different than the animals by giving man a soul and the free will to make decisions for himself (Genesis 1:27). God has wanted man to be with Him, BUT only if man wanted to be there. God's wonderful gift of free will allows man to make decisions independently based on his own choices. Man's desire to be with God is evident when he follows God's commandments. God knew that men would need a way to please God even when they made mistakes following His commandments. He had a plan to forgive man of these mistakes before the beginning of time with foreknowledge of man's failing, choices, and actions.

In Romans 8, we learn that God purposely predetermined this plan to allow man to use his free will to choose to follow God. *"And we know that all things work together for good to those who love God, to those who are the called according to*

His purpose. For whom He foreknew, He also predestined to be conformed to the image of His Son, that He might be the firstborn among many brethren. Moreover whom He predestined, these He also called; whom He called, these He also justified; and whom He justified, these He also glorified" (Romans 8:28-30). These verses tell us that God decided in the beginning how man could be acceptable to Him. He planned before time began and people that answer God's call to obey His commandments are justified and glorified by being with God in heaven.

When you realize that God is God and made the endless universe, how hard is it to understand that God can know what He is going to do before He starts? God made everything with all the beauty and grandeur and detail that we see every day. It should not be a reach for us to understand that when God made us with free will, He didn't want robots, but people who gladly worshipped Him of their own choosing. God treats all people who follow His plan as sons and daughters and provides them with spiritual blessings (Ephesians 1:3-4). If He had wanted robot followers, He would have made those. God's predetermination assures us of a way to be holy with God as His adopted family, because we want to be a member of His family.

God's providence is active in our lives today. The most important element of God's care is the plan of salvation that we know today. God provides what we need in our daily lives, makes Himself available to us in prayer, and is a constant presence in our lives. God has provided for man since the beginning of time and will continue to do so until the end of time. The providence of God takes care of ALL of us.

The KISS Method

Have you ever heard of the KISS Method (Keep It Simple, Stupid)? It is a common problem solving approach, but have you ever applied it to Christianity? The KISS Method is a problem solving approach that promotes the simplest approach or solution as the best. The KISS Method encourages the use of a less complicated system or procedure instead of an overly complex process.

In the Old Testament, the law of Moses was given to the Israelites. The law is specific with guidance related to food, offerings, tithes, sanctuary, debts, feasts, slaves and servants, administration of justice, community health management, priests and their duties, marriage and family relationships, and many other civil and religious matters. The law has detailed procedures for all these areas and all of the law was required to be kept to be pleasing to God. The Pharisees added to the law by making many rules to help the Jews implement and keep the law. For example, the Jews were to rest on the Sabbath day. So the Pharisees developed a rule for how far a person could walk on the Sabbath day and still be resting. Of course, all of this made a very complicated process to obey the law.

Christianity does not have all these laws, rules, and traditions. Sometime we struggle as Christians, because we don't have a rule for every aspect of our lives nor are we required to have elaborate works with intricate processes. Many of us struggle with the liberty given to us by Christ. We do not apply the KISS Method daily as we work to be strong Christians following God's word.

Naaman is an Old Testament example of someone who wanted to perform grand activities instead of following simple guidance. Naaman was a Syrian commander with leprosy. A young slave girl advised Naaman that the prophet Elisha could cure him. Elisha sent instructions to Naaman to dip in the Jordan River seven times. This simple guidance made Naaman furious! Naaman thought the Jordan River was too small and dipping in water seven times was not a grand enough act for a commander. Naaman's servants advised him saying, "*If the prophet had told you to do something great, would you not have done it?*" Of course, when Naaman followed Elisha's simple instructions, he was cured of his leprosy.

Even the first century Christians struggled with the liberties of Christianity. In Acts 15, the Jewish Christians wanted the Gentile Christians to be circumcised as was required of the Jews under the old law. These Jewish Christians wanted Christianity AND the law of Moses. The disciples had to teach Christians familiar with the Jewish law and traditions that God saved through grace, not the laws and traditions that were impossible to completely fulfill. Paul also wrote about Christian liberties in Romans 14 and 15. Paul teaches us that "*he who serves Christ in these things is acceptable to God and approved by men. Therefore let us pursue the things which make for peace and the things by which one may build up anothe*r." God did not want tension between Christians based on rules made up by man because of their personal situations. He wanted all Christians to work together for the good of all.

Is Christianity so simple, that we cannot understand what God requires of us? To be a Christian, a person must believe

in God, be baptized into Christ, and worship God as the first
century Christians did. Jesus taught us (Matthew 22:37-40)
that the greatest commandment was to love God with all you
heart, soul and mind and that the second greatest commandment was to love your neighbor as yourself. So the KISS
Method to be a Christian is to worship simply as the disciples
did during the first century and to apply God's commandments to our everyday activities. Simple Christianity does
not require ornate trappings and complicated procedures, but
simply following God's gospel plan.

Paul's Faithful Sayings

Have you ever noticed Paul's faithful sayings in his letters to Timothy and Titus? Five times in these three letters, Paul emphasizes a point by calling it a faithful saying. Is Paul repeating a proverb which is something that is usually true? Or is he using the term "faithful saying" to be sure that his point is emphasized?

Paul is telling Timothy and Titus to pay attention and learn using this writing style! All of Paul's faithful sayings are taught as always true in other books of the Bible. These are Paul's five faithful sayings.

1 Timothy 1:15 — *This is a **faithful saying** and worthy of all acceptance, that Christ Jesus came into the world to save sinners, of whom I am chief.*

1 Timothy 3:1 — *This is a **faithful saying**: If a man desires the position of a bishop, he desires a good work.*

1 Timothy 4:8-9 — *For bodily exercise profits a little, but godliness is profitable for all things, having promise of the life that now is and of that which is to come. This is a **faithful saying** and worthy of all acceptance.*

2 Timothy 2:11-13— *This is a **faithful saying**: For if we died with Him, We shall also live with Him. If we endure, we shall also reign with Him. If we deny Him, He also will deny us. If we are faithless, He remains faithful; he cannot deny Himself.*

Titus 3:8 — This is a *faithful saying*, and these things I want you to affirm constantly, that those who have believed in God should be careful to maintain good works. These things are good and profitable to men.

In Paul's first faithful saying, he is emphasizing that Christ came to save sinners. Matthew also teaches us the same lesson. In Matthew 1:21, he says, *"And she will bring forth a Son, and you shall call His name Jesus, for He will save His people from their sins."* Also in Matthew 9:13b, Matthew quotes Jesus as saying *"For I did not come to call the righteous, but sinners, to repentance."* Christ's purpose to save men is the theme throughout Romans. For example, Romans 10:13, *"For whoever calls upon the name of the Lord shall be saved"* demonstrates the Christ saves sinners.

In Paul's second faithful saying, he is emphasizing that the work of a bishop (elder) is a wonderful work for men's leadership aspirations in the church. Praise for the work of bishops can be found in other books. In 1 Peter 5:1, Peter praises the work of the elders and verifies that he is also an elder, *"The elders who are among you I exhort, I who am a fellow elder."* What an example of church leadership has Peter made for our men today! In this verse, Peter has verified the value he places for our elders (bishop) with praise and a personal illustration. Luke demonstrates the importance of the work of bishops/elders throughout the book of Acts. For example, in Acts 15, the elders of Jerusalem discuss circumcision and other requirements for new Christians. Many times in Acts, Paul confers with elders as he travels. The work of bishops/elders has been considered very important since the beginning of the church.

In Paul's third faithful saying, he is emphasizing that we must lead godly lives to have the promise of life in heaven. In Acts 10:35, Luke writes *"But in every nation whoever fears Him and works righteousness is accepted by Him."*

In Titus 2: 11-12, Paul writes, *"For the grace of God that brings salvation has appeared to all men, teaching us that, denying ungodliness and worldly lusts, we should live soberly, righteously, and godly in the present age."* In Romans 5:21b, Paul stresses that our righteousness is necessary for salvation — *"even so grace might reign through righteousness to eternal life through Jesus Christ our Lord."*

In Paul's fourth faithful saying, he is emphasizing that God if faithful and will keep all His promises, but we must live as God has directed us. In Romans 6, Paul teaches us: *"For if we have been united together in the likeness of His death, certainly we also shall be in the likeness of His resurrection."* Matthew 10:33 quotes Jesus who is teaching His apostles saying, *"Whoever denies Me before men, him I will also deny before My Father who is in heaven."* In Numbers 23:19, Moses writes, *"God is not a man, that He should lie, Nor a son of man, that He should repent. Has He said, and will He not do? Or has He spoken, and will He not make it good?"* All these verses affirm Paul's fourth faithful saying.

In Paul's fifth and last faithful saying, he is emphasizing that Christians are hard workers. In Acts 9:36, Dorcas' example is for all Christians today. *"At Joppa there was a certain disciple named Tabitha, which is translated Dorcas. This woman was full of good works and charitable deeds which she did."* In his letter to the Romans, Paul writes, *". . . but glory, honor, and peace to everyone who works what is good, to the Jew first and also to the Greek"* (Romans 2:10) to teach that good works are necessary for all Christians. For another illustration of this saying, in 1 Timothy 5:10, Paul establishes the guidelines for support by the church of Christian widows. Supported widows must be *"well reported for good works: if she has brought up children, if she has lodged strangers, if she has washed the saints' feet, if she has relieved the afflicted, if she has diligently followed every good work."* Our faith must be demonstrated by our good works. Paul is making sure that Timothy and Titus understand this.

Paul's five faithful sayings were important to Timothy and Titus and are important to us today. These sayings are not proverbs, but basic Christian teaching and general doctrine with supporting verses throughout the New Testament. Paul was emphasizing to these young men – salvation through Christ; praise for work of the elders; Christians living godly lives; God's faithfulness; and demonstration of our faith through hard work. Paul's faithful sayings are foundation doctrine for all Christians – then and now.

Is My Faith Better Than the Israelites?

I love to study the Old Testament history books. The dramatic saga of the Israelites is full of intrigue, hope, and human failings with more twists and turns than any movie thriller. In a movie thriller, the star always goes down the staircase, but should have known not to do that! The movie star can't see what is coming, because it is not in the movie script for him to know. I always wonder why the Israelites can't see the next event. They lived in a time when God spoke to the patriarchs and had specific guidance and promises from God. God had promised to bless the Israelites as long as they followed His commands, but the Israelites did not always have faith in God and His promises. I hope that my faith is better than the Israelites.

Moses has wonderful movies scenes as he leads the Israelites out of Egypt to the Promised Land. These scenes include the ten plagues that end with the eerie night where all the Egyptian first born are killed; the parting of the Red Sea during the escape from Pharaoh's chariots and soldiers; the tower of smoke and pillar of fire that leads the Israelites through the wilderness; and the manna that feeds the Israelites each day. Of course, no movie scene is better than the one where Moses is with God on Mount Sinai and receives the Ten Commandments.

All of us know the story of the Israelites as they continually doubt God. For example, Moses stays on Mount Sinai with God longer than the Israelites think is necessary. The Israelites persuade Aaron to make an idol out of the gold they had carried out of Egypt. They forget all of the wonderful things that God had done for them and begin to worship a manmade statue due to their perceived delay of Moses' return. The Israelites had seen, but forgotten, the ten plagues, the parting of the Red Sea, the tower of smoke, the pillar of fire, and the manna. Every Israelite could personally witness these evidences of God as He wasn't distant in their lives. He was a daily part of Israelite life.

Every time I am in a class studying Old Testament history, someone says, "How could the Israelites doubt God as He clearly was taking care of them?" We don't need to answer that question as much as this question, "I wonder if my faith is better that the Israelites?"

There are daily evidences of God's power and care of us today. We don't need to see the parting of the Red Sea and the lightning on Mount Sinai. We have God's word that is given to us in the Bible. God speaks to us individually, not through a patriarch. The drama of the Israelites is written for us to know the nature of God and how to follow God. We can learn from the mistakes of the Israelites and not make the same mistakes they did. We can have stronger faith by studying the Israelites.

God made promises to the Israelites. He promised that He would bless them as long as they followed His commandments and God was faithful to His promises. God has made promises to Christians today. 2 John 5 summarizes God's promises to us, "*These things I have written to you who believe in the name of the Son of God, that you may know that you have eternal life and that you may continue to believe in the name of the Son of God.*" God encourages us daily and reminds us that the things of this world are temporary and the things of heaven are eternal (2 Corinthians 18) and as Christians we must keep ourselves set apart from the world with obedience (1 Peter 1:16). Christians who believe and obey have the promise of eternal life. Remember how God told the Israelites that they had to obey His commandments to receive His blessings? Each Christian must have obedient faith to have faith better than the Israelites!

Free Choice Feeding

The first thing that everyone should know is that I am a city girl married to a farm boy. Oh, the things that I have learned about raising cattle and horses! I am so glad that my husband is patient and gives me encouragement as I learn. He frequently has to repeat what he has already told me and to help me work through my mistakes. Our cows and horses are patient also and depend on my husband and me to provide them what they need. However, it is their choice whether to take of the food and water. Believe me, the old saying is true — you can lead a horse to water, but you cannot make him drink. We take care of the cows and horses by having water and some types of food always available and some types of food offered only at certain times.

Hay and grass are provided so that they can eat whatever amount they want — when they want it. This is called free choice feeding. Cattle and horses are not called hay-burners without a reason and really eat a bunch of hay! Whether the sun is shining or the weather is cold, the cows and horses depend on the hay that we provide for them each day. The cows are so contented after eating hay. Then they rest and chew their cud as if they are contemplating life!

We also put out a mineral mixture made specifically for the cows or horses. It is also offered free choice, so that any cow or horse can eat the mixture whenever it wants to have some. Instinctively they come and eat the minerals that keep them healthy. Even the calves and colts eat the mineral when they are old enough to digest it! Who would think that the animals would know to eat this gritty mixture? But they do eat it and need it each day!

The most vivid example of free choice feeding is a cow or mare nursing its baby. I love to watch the baby grow. They grow from the spindly legged newborn to the weanling to a grown animal. As it grows, it weans from its mother's milk to the food eaten by the grown animals. It is so fun to watch the baby try hay, because its mother already enjoys the hay! No baby animal can grow to a mature animal without learning to eat what the grown animals eat.

Of course, some food is only offered at specific times. Both the cows and horses look forward to this food. I guess it is like having dessert for them. The cows moo and the horses nicker as we come into the barn to get this feed. They are so excited to have this special feeding and want us to hurry and bring it out. They certainly know when feeding time is!

There is also too much of a good thing for both the cows and horses. Some food is enticing to the animals, but could make them sick or kill them. It is our responsibility to restrict them from eating the things that would cause them harm. For example, too much spring grass makes a horse founder which is an acutely painful inflammation of the foot. Some plants that are used in landscaping could kill our animals. We must protect them from the things that could harm them while providing them the food that they need.

God has provided for us in a similar manner. God is patient with us through our many questions and mistakes as we learn to live Christian lives. God constantly provides us with advice and guidance with more patience than my husband ever could! Since the beginning of time, God has provided guidance for man. He walked in the *cool of the evening* with

Adam and Eve in the Garden of Eden. After Adam and Eve disappointed Him by eating of the Tree of Knowledge of Good and Evil, He made known His plan to provide salvation and eternal life with Him for them and the rest of mankind. The Old Testament chronicles God's many disappointments with the Israelites and how He spoke to them through the patriarchs, judges, and prophets to teach them. Then in the New Testament, God has provided His last covenant and the gospel message with guidance for us. God has been patiently guiding and teaching man since the beginning of time.

We have God's word and the gospel message as free choice feeding. God constantly provides, but it is our choice to believe the gospel message or not. Instinctively we know that we need it, but God gave us free will to decide whether to partake of His gospel plan. God has always wanted us to decide for ourselves to follow Him and obey His commandments and has never wanted robots. There is a dramatic story in Acts 26 demonstrating this. In this chapter, Paul has been a prisoner for some time and his case is being reviewed by King Agrippa. Paul's defense to Agrippa summarized how he changed from a persecutor of the Christians to a believer in Christ and the gospel. In verse 27, Paul charges Agrippa, *"I know that you do believe."* Because Agrippa had free choice, he replied to Paul, *"You almost persuade me to become a Christian."* God did not compel Agrippa to become a Christian which would have made it politically correct to be a Christian during Paul's time. It was Agrippa's choice. God is always there for us and it is our choice to eat or not.

God wants us to learn and grow into mature Christians as the baby animals wean from milk to hay. We cannot continue as babies, but must learn to live as strong Christian people. In Hebrews 5, it is written *"For though by this time you ought to be teachers, you need someone to teach you again the first principles of the oracles of God; and you have come to need milk and not solid food. For everyone who partakes only of milk is unskilled in the word of righteousness, for he is a babe. But solid food belongs to those who are of full age, that is, those who by reason of use have their senses exercised to discern both good and evil"* (5:12-14). God clearly expects us to mature as Christians, just as the calves and colts grow to mature animal; first drinking only their mother's milk and then eating hay and grain as a grown animal.

Christians also have special feedings like the animals do! We have our individual prayer time and the weekly Lord's Supper. In our prayer time, our souls are fed with peace and knowledge from God which strengthens our spiritual bodies as the special feedings strengthen our animals. Also God has provided us with the Lord's Supper to remind us that we need Him and to remember Jesus' sacrifice. We eagerly look forward to participating in this weekly communion with God. This feeding supplements our free choice feedings by giving us opportunities to build our spiritual union with God and to become stronger Christians.

God's word gives us guidance to avoid things that can harm us similar to the protection that we give our animals from too much spring grass. God warns us to not value the earthly treasures more than spiritual treasures. In Luke 12, Jesus tells the story of the rich fool that valued his vast accumulation of crops and goods. This rich fool had so much that he built bigger barns to store everything. Of course, when the rich fool thought he had everything that he would ever need, he died. Who then had the rich fool's crops and goods? They certainly weren't doing the rich fool much good as he faced God's judgment. When we feed on God's word, we learn how to avoid enticements that can harm our souls.

God has given us His gospel as free choice feeding with planned nutritional supplements and restrictions. Each individual decides whether to follow God's gospel plan or not. That is our free will and the free choice feeding for our soul!

Thoroughly Modern

We are proud to be thoroughly modern as we live our twenty-first century lives. We do not struggle as people did in ancient times when they lived in caves chasing mastodons for their next meal. We survived the Y2K crisis with our computer programs and electronic data intact. Our lives are enriched with instant communications and fast food. We live comfortable lives and worry about losing excess weight! Keeping up with modern advances and fads can become our priority and our old-fashioned God often takes a back burner.

What is considered to be modern has evolved through the ages. Civilization has moved from hunter/gatherer to agricultural to technological. In the beginning of time, man had a predominantly migratory lifestyle with practical knowledge of the environment and food sources. As agricultural knowledge grew, there was an increased dependence on plants and animal husbandry which led to cities and more industrial development. Technological improvements made life easier for man as he created specialized products and tools to perform tasks.

Modern has changed with the ages as man strove to use the newest technique, tool or technology. Ancient Polynesians had an extensive knowledge of navigation that allowed them to sail on the ocean to specific islands and fishing spots. Ancient Egyptians used complex engineering methods that cannot be duplicated today to build the pyramids. Mayans of Central America developed a sophisticated mathematics that calculated in units of 20. Babylonians living over 4,200 years ago developed Cuneiform, the first form of writing. The invention of the printing press produced the Gutenberg Bible in 1455. The steam engine was invented in the mid 18th century which led to many industrial improvements for the production of goods. Modern civilization grew on parallel paths for people across our earth with unique techniques, tools, and knowledge for each group.

What is modern depends on the point in the timeline and the group of people that are being considered. While men change what is deemed to be modern, God has been the same throughout the timeline. God is the same today when we drive down the highway with our cell phones in our ears as when He created the universe. Having an eternal God means that when man was learning to gather wild wheat at the beginning of time to today when man harvests wheat with a huge mechanical combine, God is the same.

When Moses asked God what to tell the captive Israelites when they asked the name of who sent Moses to rescue them, God told Moses to reply, *"Thus you shall say to the children of Israel, 'I AM has sent me to you.'"* Paul writes (Romans 1:20a), *"For since the creation of the world His invisible attributes are clearly seen, being understood by the things that are made, even His eternal power and Godhead."* Our God is eternal and steadfast. The I AM loved man when He created him and loves man today. While we are enjoying our modern comforts and conveniences, remember God is the same today as when man chased mastodons.

Lifestyle

Learning From Martha

Have you ever studied the character of Martha in the New Testament to see if you are like her? Martha is the sister of Mary and Lazarus and is often overshadowed by them. We know that Jesus loved them all, but sometimes we don't really understand Martha as well as we understand Mary and Lazarus. However, we know a lot about Martha and we can learn a lot from her.

First let's look at what Luke 10 tells us about Martha.

> Now it happened as they went that He (Jesus) entered a certain village; and a certain woman named Martha welcomed Him into her house. And she had a sister called Mary, who also sat at Jesus' feet and heard His word. But Martha was distracted with much serving, and she approached Him and said, "Lord, do You not care that my sister has left me to serve alone? Therefore tell her to help me." And Jesus answered and said to her, "Martha, Martha, you are worried and troubled about many things. But one thing is needed, and Mary has chosen that good part, which will not be taken away from her" (10:38-42).

In this story, Martha is not a shining example, but is very much like most of us. Martha is striving to be hospitable, the perfect hostess with the perfect home, the perfect food, and the perfect ambiance. Doesn't that sound familiar? Often we worry that our hospitality isn't perfect, so we don't invite people into our homes. We are afraid that our living room is not clean enough or nice enough. We worry that our food will not be good. Notice that Mary had relaxed and was enjoying the company in her home! Most people enjoy the opportunity to socialize in your home and are not worried about the stain on the carpet. Be realistic and know that sometimes dust will be in the corner and the food will not be gourmet. This story shows us that we shouldn't be like Martha and worry about things that don't matter. Be like Mary and relax, enjoy the company in your home and maybe you will entertain angels!

Now let's look at what John 11 tells us about Martha. For context, preceding this reading, Lazarus had been sick and was dead four days when Jesus arrives. Martha goes out to meet Jesus and his apostles on the road.

> Now Martha said to Jesus, "Lord, if You had been here, my brother would not have died. But even now I know that whatever You ask of God, God will give You." Jesus said to her, "Your brother will rise again." Martha said to Him, "I know that he will rise again in the resurrection at the last day." Jesus said to her, "I am the resurrection and the life. He who believes in Me, though he may die, he shall live. And whoever lives and believes in Me shall never die. Do you believe this?" She said to Him, "Yes, Lord, I believe that You are the Christ, the Son of God, who is to come into the world."

Now this is the Martha to be! Her confession of faith is so wonderful and made during a very difficult time in her life. I am always amazed at how clearly Martha understands that Jesus is the Christ when she could not have known or comprehended the full gospel message. With her confession, she clearly states her faith in Jesus based on what she knew at that time. Our faith has the benefit of the Bible and the full revelation of the mystery of God. She had wanted Jesus to heal Lazarus and was now certain that she will see Lazarus again in heaven. Martha's faith in Jesus is clear and unshakeable. Can you imagine Martha's glee when Jesus raises Lazarus on that day? All of us should strive to have faith like Martha!

The third reading for Martha is in John 12:1-2.

> Then, six days before the Passover, Jesus came to Bethany, where Lazarus was who had been dead, whom He had raised from the dead. There they made Him a supper; and Martha served, but Lazarus was one of those who sat at the table with Him.

In this reading, Jesus knows His time on the cross is soon and the fellowship of Martha and her family provide Him with fellowship and love. Clearly enjoying the company of brethren strengthens everyone. The time that we spend in fellowship with our brethren provide us with support and brotherhood. Hospitality and fellowship strengthen all Christians in our everyday lives and as we face hardships. In this reading, Martha is teaching us to look for opportunities to fellowship with other Christians.

So what have we learned from Martha? First, enjoy the opportunities that we have to be hospitable. Don't worry about the small stuff. Enjoy your guests and ignore the dust bunnies. Second, have faith. Martha's faith in Jesus is clear and she based her actions on her faith. We may not be the best Bible scholar or know everything there is to know about the gospel. However, our faith that Jesus is Christ should be as strong as Martha's faith. Third, fellowship strengthens Christians. We should reach out to other Christians and stand ready to support others who are having a difficult time.

Martha can teach us a lot and all of us should learn from Martha!

The Now Generation

The Now Generation is a term describing a segment of the U.S. population and culture. The Now Generation seeks immediate excitement, is not tolerant of boredom, is not satisfied with old standards, seeks pleasure for themselves, and knows good times are coming. People of the Now Generation think they have the most current and unique approaches to life and life's problems. Their attitude demands the good things of life now without the responsibility or authority for the demands. The lyrics of a contemporary song demonstrate the attitude of the Now Generation.

> *" It was a now generation*
> *And I just can't wait*
> *I need it immediately*
> *And I just can't wait*
> *I want it immediately."*

> *"cause time can't wait*
> *And I sure can't wait*
> *I ain't got no patience*
> *No, I sure can't wait, not today."* *

Moses had this same problem with the Israelites as he was leading them out of Egypt. For example, Moses was on Mount Sinai for forty days and nights with the Lord to receive the law and commandments of God (Exodus 24:12-18). Moses had told the Israelites to go to Aaron if they had any problems. It wasn't long before the Israelites did go to Aaron! They were impatient and did not want to wait on God and Moses any longer. They wanted a god to worship, to take care of them, and to give them the things that they had in Egypt. They wanted a god who they could see and touch and they wanted it now! We know the rest of the story. Aaron built a golden calf for the Israelites to worship knowing it was the wrong thing to do. The Israelites were dancing and worshipping the golden calf when Moses came down from the mountain. The Israelites were impatient and wanted immediate gratification for their desires. They had no authority to make a golden idol and every responsibility to follow their Lord God. This isn't the only example of the Israelites' impatience, as the Old Testament is full of the Israelite attitude. The Israelites of old were definitively part of the Now Generation mind set.

The Old Testament also has wonderful examples of people who waited for God. God made promises to three patriarchs, Abraham, Isaac, and Jacob. Each of these patriarchs lived his life believing that God would fulfill these promises without knowing when or how they would be fulfilled. They were not a member of the Now Generation, as they patiently waited on God. Of course, we know this story too. The promises were that God would make a great nation of their descendents, that this nation would have land, and that through this nation all nations would be blessed. Their descendents became a great nation while living in Egypt. This great nation of Israelites conquered and lived in the land of Canaan. All nations were blessed with the birth of Christ who was a descendent of Abraham, Isaac, and Jacob. These promises were made to the patriarchs, but God fulfilled them according to His timetable, not for the immediate gratification of the patriarchs. These great leaders did not live their lives for self-gratification, but to please God and follow His commandments. They knew that *"with the Lord one day is as a thousand years, and a thousand years as one day"* and that God's commandments were greater than their personal desires.

Simon, the sorcerer was a first century Christian who had the same mindset as the Now Generation (Acts 8:9-25). Simon had previously practiced sorcery, but was taught and baptized by Philip. Simon was used to astonishing the people of Samaria and claiming that he was someone great. Simon clearly was an exciting man to know and made fun times for the Samaritan citizens! Simon offered money to the apostles for spiritual gifts, because he wanted to continue to be a great man and amaze the crowds! Simon was only seeking pleasure and instant gratification; he was chastised for not having his heart right in the sight of God.

However, the rest of the story for Simon is a wonderful example of how NOT to be a Now Generation Christian. In verse 24, Simon says, *"Pray to the Lord for me, that none of the things which you have spoken may come upon me."* Simon recognized that the Now Generation attitude was not the proper one for a Christian. He understood that his hope of heaven was not an earthly hope and taught the gospel to many Samaritans with his godly understanding. Simon was NOT a Now Generation Christian.

A Christian's hope is spiritual life in heaven with God. In 2 Timothy 4:8, Paul writes, *"Finally, there is laid up for me the crown of righteousness, which the Lord, the righteous Judge, will give to me on that Day, and not to me only but also to all who have loved His appearing."* God has the authority for His provided commandments and all Christians have the responsibility to live by the commandments. Even though we live here on earth and want a big house with a nice car that is not what God has promised us. Our modern culture requires all these things for a person to be considered successful and happy. However, the Bible teaches us to be quiet in our soul and to wait on God (Psalm 62:5) the very opposite of the Now Generation attitude.

Today as Christians, we must not be part of the Now Generation. Hebrews 11:1 says *"faith is the substance of things hoped for, the evidence of things not seen."* Christians' earnest expectation of heaven and the fulfillment of all God's promises is the standard for our daily living. This hope does not mean that we will get our dream job with the biggest home in town as the Now Generation would expect. Our hope is modeled after the Old Testament patriarchs and strengthened by the first century Christians. Christians wait patiently on God, knowing that God has promised all good things to us spiritually. These song lyrics demonstrate a better attitude for a Christian.

The Lord is my light and my salvation.
Whom shall I fear?
And He is my strength, the defense of my life,
Whom shall I fear?
Have mercy, O Lord and answer my cry.
Turn not away.
For Thou art my help,
The God of salvation.
Turn not away.

Chorus
Wait, wait, O wait on the Lord.
Be strong and take courage!
Wait on the Lord.
Wait, wait, O wait on the Lord,
Be strong and take courage!
Yes, wait on the Lord.**

*Song by the Black Eyed Peas titled "The Now Generation"

** Song titled "The Lord is My Light" by C. E. Couchman and published in *Hymns for Worship (Supplement)*

Does He Leak out Our Edges?

Recently someone told me about a conversation he had with a child. The child asked my friend, "Is God really bigger than all of us?" My friend answered, "Yes." The child asked "And He lives inside us?" My friend again answered, "Yes." The child then asked, "Well, does He leak out our edges?"

Does God leak out our edges? Only a child would ask that question. However, maybe we should ask "Does God leak out MY edges?" or "Can others see God in me?"

The child is not wrong in her conclusion. God should leak out our edges! Others should be able to see God in us by how we live our lives and the things that we do. In the Sermon on the Mount (Matthew 5:16), Jesus said, *"Even so, let your light shine before men; that they may see your good works, and glorify your Father who is in heaven."* This light is how other people can see God "leaking out our edges." When our motive is to show glory to God and not to show how great we are, our good works let God "leak out our edges."

The apostles let God "leak out their edges." Their faith in God was so strong that they taught both Jew and Gentile about Jesus at every opportunity. One time, Peter and John had been jailed by Jewish leaders for preaching in Jerusalem. They were commanded not to speak or teach in the name of Jesus. Peter and John told those Jewish leaders that they had to do what God said and not man! When they were released, they continued to preach about Jesus! (Acts 4:13-21). God was certainly "leaking out" Peter and John's edges while they were preaching and teaching in Jerusalem.

Another time Paul and Silas were in stocks in a Philippian jail after being beaten. While in the stocks, Paul and Silas were praying and singing! Of course, the other prisoners and jailers were listening to them. They all knew of Paul and Silas' faith in Jesus by the heartfelt singing (Acts 16: 23-30). I bet such singing was not common in a Philippian jail where death was a more common reality. God was certainly "leaking out" their edges and all they were doing was praying and singing.

A wonderful disciple named Tabitha also let God "leak out." Her story is in Acts 9:36-42. Verse 36 tells us, *"This woman was full of good works and acts of mercy."* Tabitha sewed clothes for widows and performed many other charitable deeds. Tabitha let others see how a Christian should treat others by taking care of other Christian widows. Tabitha let her light shine and God "leaked out" her edges for all the people of Joppa to see. Tabitha did not perform miraculous works – she just did what she could do!

Today each of us can let others see God by how we treat and help others. The way that we act each day shows our faith in God and gives Him glory. In 1 Peter 2:12, Peter tells us, *"they may by your good works, which they see, glorify God."* At that time, the early Christians were facing severe persecution from the pagan world. These Christians abstained from immorality and other pagan rites. They worked together to help each other in these severe situations and to teach others about Christianity. When the pagans saw these works from the early Christians, it brought glory to God. In other words, when we help others in the most noble and pure sense, God "leaks out" of us.

So we need to take the advice of this child — let our light shine so that God "leaks out our edges"! We can do this with simple everyday living. As we live as Christians and find opportunities to do what God says, we must use those occasions to teach, sing, and work for God's glory. People around us will see God's glory in our activities and He will be "leaking out our edges"!

Living a Peaceable Life

The Bible teaches us to live a quiet and peaceable life. The dictionary defines "peaceable" as "disposed to peace, not contentious or quarrelsome, quietly behaved or marked by freedom from strife or disorder." It must have been easy to have a quiet and peaceable life in Bible times, but how can we do that today?

The first point to be made is it was not easy to have a quiet and peaceable life in Bible times. Throughout Bible history, upheavals, war, and change were as evident and widespread as today. King David had spent his whole life at war and due to the blood on his hands, God did not allow David to build His temple. God wanted His people to learn to be quiet on the inside — no matter what was happening on the outside. David knew this and wrote, *"Surely I have calmed and quieted my soul, like a weaned child with its mother"* (Psalm 131:2). David had learned not to be anxious, but to lean quietly upon God as a child leans on its mother. God blessed Solomon, David's son, with peace and quietness (1 Chronicles 22:9) and allowed Solomon to build His temple. This period was markedly different from the years before Solomon.

Living a quiet and peaceable life starts with the individual as he learns to be quiet and peaceable within himself. Paul writes to the Thessalonians, *"that you aspire to lead a quiet life, to mind your own business"* (1 Thessalonians 4:11) and *"that they work in quietness and eat their own bread"* (2 Thessalonians 3:12).

Leading a quiet life free from strife and disorder is not desirable for a lot of people in contemporary society. Our culture emphasizes flash and dash and does not value the components of life that make life worthwhile. Remember the joke on the tombstone – "I wish I had spent more time at the office"? That summarizes today's culture and goals and not God's goal for us. God wants each person to be calm within himself and apply God's word to his daily life. With this personal restraint and daily practice, the person can live a peaceable life as described in the Bible.

Living a peaceable life is also a goal for our church family. The book of 1 Corinthians is full of guidance for the church family (for example, no division among brethren is in the first chapter). The church is not to be a contentious place where each person seeks prominence over others. James 3:17, tells us that *the wisdom that is from above is first pure, then peaceable, gentle, willing to yield, full of mercy and good fruits, without partiality and without hypocrisy.*" All Christians have different abilities that are all needed to help our church family have a peaceable life. We are to work together in a cooperative spirit to achieve the work of the church.

Living a peaceable life under a government is also a requirement of Christians. 1 Timothy 2:2 teaches us to pray *"for kings and all in authority, that we may lead a quiet and peaceable life in all godliness and reverence."* Many people today and in Bible times lived under harsh rulers. In a recent newspaper article, the author believed Americans were praying for an easy life and to be left alone when they prayed for peace. Being a Christian does not guarantee an easy life or that the Christian will not be involved in government events. Christians are to pray for our leaders and to follow God first as we strive to live a godly life.The purpose of the Bible is not to have a Christian government, but to live as a Christian under a government.

Living a peaceable life encompasses all aspects of a Christian's life. It is not harder to live a peaceable life now than it was in Bible times, it is just different. The Christian must learn to have a peaceable life by learning to be calm within himself and leaning on God. This quiet attitude is applied as the Christian works within his church family and within his government. By living a quiet and peaceable life, a Christian can have influence on everyone! Our motto can be this verse from Philippians 4:11, *"Not that I speak in regard to need, for I have learned in whatever state I am, to be content."*

Jordan's Three Rules of Management

I worked as a manager for many years and, as I became more experienced, I had opportunity to give guidance to younger managers. I had three rules that I gave to these young managers. To a Christian, these three rules are not a surprise at all. However, many have not considered how Christian principles are relevant to corporate life. My three rules of management were:

- Don't lie, cheat, or steal (counts as one rule!)
- Don't say anything that you don't want repeated
- Treat others as you would like to be treated

Followers of corporate situation ethics would disparage my first rule of management (Don't lie, cheat or steal). Situation ethics classes teach students to identify circumstances where moral values can be redefined. After all, current corporate managers often lie, cheat and steal and then have business awards for their successes and magazine articles written about their life. Our corporate culture loves a winner! A Christian manager cannot redefine moral values based on a business situation. In Acts 5, Ananias and Sapphira apply situational ethics when they lie about the value of land they had sold. Ananias and Sapphira wanted the accolades from fellow Christians for donating the full value received from the sale of their land. However, they did not want to really donate the full land value. So they kept part of the money from the sale and told everyone a lesser price from the sale of the land. They donated this lesser price to the work of the church and God struck them dead for their lie. Situational ethics does not work! My first management rule (don't lie, cheat or steal) does work!

My second management rule (Don't say anything that you don't want repeated) has broad application for a Christian manager. We all know that people like to gossip and talk about others in their workplace. Proverbs 20:19 tell us, "*A gossip betrays a confidence; so avoid a man who talks too much.*" It is not always bad to talk about others, but it is easy to cross the line into gossip. Often we are talking about others for our entertainment and to make ourselves seem better than another person. In the corporate and other personal environments, conversations are often repeated and not necessarily repeated with accuracy. Our words must always reflect the highest integrity and be able to withstand scrutiny when others repeat our words. Remember, you cannot swallow your words after you have spoken them!

My third rule of management (Treat others as you would like to be treated) was taught by Jesus in the Sermon on the Mount (Matthew 5:43-47). In this sermon, Jesus tells us to love both our neighbors and our enemies. He teaches that anyone can be nice to those who are nice to him. He wants Christians to treat everyone like they want to be treated – including your enemies. This biblical guidance is directly applicable to every aspect of our corporate culture! All of us are better managers when we follow Jesus' teachings. Our teams also have more confidence in leaders who have real concern about the team members.

Over time, these young managers have become my friends and peers. Sometimes they laughingly ask me if I still remember my three rules of management. Well, I know the rules and now you know them too.

Beauty

Physical beauty has a profound impact in contemporary society. We are bombarded with physically attractive people in all media with the message that each of us should aspire to be as beautiful as these people. Throughout history, our literature and art are filled with images of physical beauty. A University of Maryland study (22 May 07) proved that even being associated with a beautiful person made a more favorable impression to the viewer. Human beings are obsessed with beauty, so what does the Bible teach us?

The Bible has many characters with physical beauty. Solomon describes in detail the beauty of the Shulamite woman in the Song of Solomon and she worries about being beautiful enough to please Solomon. Sarai was so beautiful that Pharaoh took her into his house and gave many gifts to Abram for her. Abram had lied and did not tell Pharaoh that Sarai was his wife, because he was afraid that Pharaoh would murder him to obtain the beautiful Sarai (Genesis 12:11-16). Esther and other young women were given beauty treatments so that King Ahasuerus could pick one of them for his new queen (Esther 2:3-9). There are also handsome men in the Bible. Saul is described as *"a choice and handsome young man...not a more handsome person than he among the children of Israel"* (1 Samuel 9:2). David is described as *"ruddy, with bright eyes, and good-looking"* (1 Samuel 16:12). Beautiful people were as appreciated in Old Testament times as they are today!

However, the Bible teaches us not to value beauty above virtues, such as, faith, righteousness, honor, and good works. Throughout the Bible, Christians are taught to be righteous, faithful and godly. We are not to value physical beauty over inner beauty and strength of character. The book of Proverbs contains many of these lessons.

Proverbs 6:25 — "Do not lust after her beauty in your heart."

Proverbs 31:30 — "Charm is deceitful and beauty is passing."

Proverbs 11:16 — "A gracious woman retains honor."

Proverbs 11:18 — "to him who sows righteousness will be a sure reward."

Proverbs 11:27 — "He who diligently seeks good finds favor."

Proverbs 12:5 — "The thoughts of the righteous are right."

Proverbs 20:11 — "Even a child is known by his deeds."

There are wonderful lessons to learn from the beautiful people in the Bible. The Song of Solomon has lessons for couples today to show them how to communicate and show concern for each other as Solomon and the Shulamite woman did. Abram and Sarai are given new names by God (Abraham and Sarah) in Genesis 17 as He promises to make Abraham a great nation and to make a new covenant with him. Abraham and Sarah were beautiful people who were faithful servants of God. In Hebrews 11, their faith that God would keep His promises is an example to us today. As queen, beautiful Esther risked her life and was brave as she pleaded for her people to save them from annihilation. Her spiritual strength stopped King Ahasuerus from killing all the Jewish people in his kingdom. The lesson for us from these beautiful people is to believe God keeps His promises even when we do not understand how it can be possible.

Of course, David is a wonderful example of beauty as the Bible tells us that David was a man after God's own heart. Reading the psalms written by David is poignant evidence of David's love for God. His faith and dependence on God are in so many psalms that it is hard to pick a favorite. David cries for God's help and deliverance can be summarized in Psalms 3:8, "*Salvation belongs to the Lord.*" His appreciation and dependence for God's care is evident in Psalms 18, "*The Lord is my rock and my fortress and my deliverer; My God, my strength, in whom I will trust. . . . I will call upon the Lord, who is worthy to be praised.*" This theme is expressed by David so many times. David may have been beautiful on the outside; however, his inner beauty shows us how to live godly lives that are pleasing to God.

Saul is an example of a beautiful person who did not please God. At first Saul attracted people due to his physical appearance. Saul did not follow God's instructions and his lack of faith in God caused Israel to be given to another kingly line. Saul is an example of a beautiful person not demonstrating righteousness and faith in God.

In the New Testament, we don't know about the beauty of the individuals whose stories and teachings are written there. For example, John the Baptist is described as wearing camel's hair, having uncut hair and living in the desert. This is not a physically appealing description – more a smelly description. The people were supposed to listen to his teaching and to be prepared for what was to come, not become fascinated with his looks. John preached, "*There comes One after me who is mightier than I, whose sandal strap I am not worthy to stoop down and loose.*" With these powerful words, what did it matter what John looked like? Another New Testament example of spiritual beauty is Paul. In 2 Corinthians 12, Paul boasts of his infirmities and teaches that God's strength is made perfect in our weakness. His writings teach each of us how to be Christians and to build our faith in God. Paul did not let his infirmities stop him from traveling and preaching throughout the Roman Empire. At the end of his life, Paul writes, *"I have fought the good fight, I have finished the race, I have kept the faith. Finally, there is laid up for me the crown of righteousness, which the Lord, the righteous Judge, will give to me on that Day."* Paul teaches us that our physical persona is not what God values, but the inner strength and faith that each of us gives to God.

Jesus came to earth as the son of a Galilean carpenter instead of a prestigious individual in order to teach us about inner beauty and godly faith. Jesus' Sermon on the Mount (Matthew 5-7) does not exalt physical beauty, but teaches us about spiritual and inner beauty. Jesus tells us, *"Blessed are the pure in heart for they shall see God"* (Matthew 5:8). He also tells us to *"not worry about . . . your body"* (Matthew 6:25), but to *"seek first the kingdom of God and His righteousness and all these things shall be added to you"* (Matthew 6:33). He taught His apostles to serve others by washing their feet, which was a duty of a slave. Jesus wanted beautiful people, all right! He wanted us to be beautiful on the inside with strength, honor, faith, and righteousness.

Physical beauty is praised in contemporary society and has been throughout the centuries. However, inner beauty should be the beauty that Christians seek. Our goal should be to be known for our godly living and not for our physical beauty.

Situational Ethics

Until I started working on this article, I thought situational ethics was a business phenomenon to justify any means to an end. Imagine my surprise to learn that the situational ethics theory is from Joseph Fletcher, an Episcopal priest, who wrote a book titled *Situation Ethics – the New Morality* in 1966! Mr. Fletcher felt the each individual must have respect for the laws, may often follow the laws and be informed by tradition. However, the individual is free to make the right choice according to the situation, because that individual would be seeking his neighbor's best interest with "goodwill at work in partnership with reason." The individual is acting out of love for others and trying to do the best to serve the interests of those other people. Mr. Fletcher taught that following rules wasn't the same thing as doing the right thing. The four principles of his theory are pragmatism, relativism, positivism, and personalism. Well, all of us know that Solomon said there is nothing new under the sun (Ecclesiastes 1:9), so what does the Bible teach about this theory?

First let us add some detail to four principles of situational ethics. Pragmatism means that for a course of action to be right, it has to be practical and must work. Relativism means that absolutes do not always apply, but depend on the situation. Positivism means that the individual must want to do good. Personalism means that rules shouldn't be put before people.

Let's apply situational ethics to the story of Aaron and the golden calf (Exodus 32:1-6). Moses had left Aaron in charge and was gone a long time on Mount Sinai. The Israelite nation was so tired and became afraid after Moses' long absence. They thought Moses wasn't coming back and asked Aaron to make them a god. They needed a god to help them in their desperate situation and fell back on their experiences relating to Egyptian idols. Aaron was in a tough spot with an angry mob and no Moses! Aaron was brave when together Moses and he were facing down the Pharaoh, but the scared Israelites caused him to apply situational ethics. Aaron applied personalism by allowing the people to choose another god when they became afraid. He was putting the Israelite nation first! He wanted to do good and make the Israelite nation feel better about their situation which is positivism. He was pragmatic when he asked them to break off their golden earrings to get the materials for the idol. Aaron was thinking relatively when he let the Israelites have any other idol before God to appease the Israelites in their desperate situation.

The Pharisees often applied situational ethics and Mark 7:1-16 is an excellent example. In this passage Jesus chided the Pharisees for creating a loophole instead of supporting parents in their old age. Tradition allowed the grown children to free themselves from the requirement to financially support their aged parents by saying, "*Whatever profit you might have received from me is Corban*" (or dedicated to the temple). Once the person said the above, he could not recall the gift (Corban) and did not have to provide any financial support for his parents. The Jewish teachings declared that it was more important to dedicate property to God than to provide for the needs of the parents. This tradition was pragmatic in that the tradition allowed the children to get rid of a duty to support their aged parents with a pious gift to the temple. The tradition was relative in that the person got to decide whether they wanted to apply this particular tradition or to provide financial support for his aged parents depending on one's parental relationship. The tradition was positivism in that the Pharisees considered gifts to God to be more important than providing financial support to aged parents. And finally the tradition is personalism in that the person was not deprived of his property while he was alive, but kept his gift until his death when it would then be given to the temple.

In both these examples, the people were not following the will of God, but performing their desired course of action to their own satisfaction. This should never be a Christian's goal!

Aaron was wrong in so many ways. Aaron was acting out of love for the Israelites. After all, they were scared and thought Moses and God had left them in the desert. Not once in the story does Aaron ask God for help. Instead of doing what God wanted, Aaron did what the people wanted and built the golden idol. Jewish tradition allows that Aaron did not willingly make the idol and asked for the gold to slow the mob down. If this was Aaron's plan, he certainly was mistaken as the Israelites quickly broke the gold from their bodies and gave it to Aaron. Aaron was a weak leader and a poor representative of God's will to the Israelites. He thinks he is making a reasonable choice in this situation, but he is following the people's wishes – not God's will.

The Pharisees could be the best group for situational ethics ever! The Pharisees made their traditions with the best interests of the Jews in mind and to help every Jew be more righteous. Often these traditions became more important than God's commandments. What they forgot was that God's will was more important than man's will EVERY time! Jesus scolds them saying, "*For laying aside the commandment of God, you hold the tradition of men*" (Mark 7:8). He is telling them that they were keeping man's tradition and ignoring God's commandments. Could this be us too?

Christians cannot be supporters of situational ethics. A Christian must make choices that seek our neighbor's best interest, but these choices must follow God's will. A person subscribing to the principles of situational ethics is putting himself above God's will.

Church of Your Choice

In the 1950s, the slogan, "Attend the Church of Your Choice," was used to get people to attend church and was part of marketing the ideal family during that era. Families were becoming more prosperous and beginning to have more entertainment choices, such as, television and AM radio. Rock and Roll was viewed as scandalous by most adults and so morality slogans were developed. Sometimes we still see the above slogan, but not as often anymore.

Today there are many church buildings that house all types of religious groups on any highway in any city. If someone wanted to attend the church of his choice, there are certainly many choices! How would this individual know which church to pick?

People in New Testament times had a similar problem. In Acts 17, Paul was traveling in Athens and finds temples to many gods throughout the city. Athenians and philosophers met in Athens to discuss new religious and spiritual ideas and spent all their time *"in nothing else, but either to tell or to hear some new thing."* The Athenian definitely had a problem choosing the church of his choice, as the city was filled with temples! They brought Paul to the Areopagus which was a semi-circle of stone seats that rose around the speaker. While standing there, Paul could look past his audience and see the bustling market and many grand temples for the idols of the citizens. There the Athenians demanded that

Paul explain the strange things that he had been teaching in the synagogue and marketplace.

The Athenians strived to be as politically correct as people strive today. Even though they had temples to all their gods, they also had one *"To the Unknown God."* (You know, just in case they were wrong or were missing one!) Paul used this temple to begin his sermon to them. He told them the many gods they worshipped were wrong, but they should worship the One True God who made everything, including them. Paul said God was not made by a man's hand, but man was made by God. Paul explained to them that there was only one God and that God commanded them to repent from their idol worshipping and follow Him. Most of the Athenians scoffed at Paul and continued to follow their many gods. Some men did repent and followed the One True God after being taught by Paul. Those Athenians found the church of God's choice on that day!

Today many of our religious groups are made by men. They created doctrine to add to the Bible and teach it as fundamental guidance from God. This doctrine is often the foundation of the group. God told us in Deuteronomy 12:32 *"Whatever I command you, be careful to observe it; you shall not add to it nor take away from it."* With that clear instruction from God, why would we want to be like the Athenians and choose a church following doctrine that was created by men?

The church of your choice must be the church that God chooses. This church is the one that we read about in the New Testament and follows His gospel plan. God is not looking for followers of man's doctrines that added to His gospel plan. In Matthew 7:21, Jesus teaches, *"Not everyone who says to Me, 'Lord, Lord,' shall enter the kingdom of heaven, but he who does the will of My Father in heaven."* Follow God's plan and attend the church of God's choice!

Works

Who Are the Workers?

Who are the workers in your local church? For sure, it must be the gifted speakers, song leaders, and teachers. After all, those functions are needed to have a worship service. It is nice to relax and enjoy the service, because you are not one of those workers. Then you get the benefits of an inspirational service without any stress! After all, Jesus and the Apostles (with the big "A" meaning the chosen twelve apostles) did the teaching and leading in the New Testament. Those early Christians could just wait on them to do all the work necessary to get the early church going – WRONG.

In his letter to the Romans, Paul (Apostle with a big "A") documents that the church is made up of many workers. Men, women, old, and young are greeted with a note of appreciation for their hard work within the church. Phoebe, a woman, is greeted as a *"helper of many."* Mary, Urbanus, Tryphena, Tryphosa, and Persis (both men and women) are all greeted as laborers and fellow workers. Whole households (of Narcissus and Aristobulus) that would include servants, children, men, and women were greeted as workers of the first century church. Paul greets Priscilla and Aquilla as *"fellow workers"* who *"risked their own necks"* for Paul's life. Andronicus and Junia are greeted as Christian workers and fellow prisoners. All of Paul's letters have similar acknowledgements of workers and emphasizes that the early church required ALL the early Christians to be workers.

Throughout the book of Acts are stories of regular people performing a wide range of tasks to help and teach other Christians. Dorcas made clothes for needy widows in Joppa. Simon, a tanner whose house was by the sea, hosted Peter during the time of Peter's vision of the clean and unclean animals. Lydia sold purple dye in Philippi and hosted Paul and Luke at her house. Luke, a Greek physician, traveled with Paul teaching the gospel throughout the known world and wrote two books of the Bible (Luke and Acts). Priscilla and Aquilla were tentmakers and taught many early Christians in Ephesus, Corinth, and Rome. Jason's house in Thessalonica was attacked, because of his association with Paul and Luke. Cornelius, a Roman centurion, taught and baptized his household. Joses' name was changed to Barnabas, meaning "son of consolation," because of the encouragement he gave to the apostles. Ananias was a Christian in Damascus who taught Saul how to be a Christian when Saul was the most feared Pharisee persecuting the early Christians. We are not specifically told everyone's profession, but the point is the early Christians did the tasks that they could do. The workers of the early church were men and women, professionals and laborers, rich and poor, Jew and Gentile.

In the Sermon on the Mount, Jesus teaches us to "*do good to those who hate you*" (Matthew 5:44). Wouldn't some type of activity be required to *"do good"?* In the beginning of the next chapter (Matthew 6:1-4), Jesus tells us to do charitable deeds without seeking personal glory. Again, isn't Jesus telling us to do good deeds? Doing good deeds is required of each Christian, not just the church leaders.

In Titus 3:8, Paul urges all Christians to work hard as this is important to their salvation. *"This is a faithful saying, and these things I want you to affirm constantly, that those who have believed in God should be careful to maintain good works. These things are good and profitable to men."* Being a Christian worker is how to have a holy life and to be set apart for God. These works can be anything that is upright and honest and demonstrates to others a Christian lifestyle and attitude. Similarly, in Galatians 6:10, Paul writes *"Therefore, as we have opportunity, let us do good to all, especially to those who are of the household of faith."* Again Paul is demonstrating that good works are part of being a Christian and required of all Christians.

In Philippians 2:12, Paul writes, *"work out your own salvation with fear and trembling."* He is teaching us that our faith is our own responsibility and we are required to demonstrate our faith with good works. He does not specifically tell each Christian what his good works must be. It is each Christian's responsibility to look for his own opportunities and to perform the good works that he can complete. God knows that each of us is different as He made us! However, He does expect us to use the talents and opportunities that we have and to be hard workers!

Getting Started

Isn't the hardest part of any project, the getting started part? It isn't hard to make a list of things to do, but it is surely harder to start working down the list. Sometimes telling others about God is just one of the things on our list. The getting started part to learning the plan of salvation is Step 1 – Hearing. There are at least two things involved in this first step. To hear the plan of salvation, someone has to talk and someone has to listen.

All of us intend to tell others of God's salvation plan; we just haven't gotten started yet. Sometimes we forget that God doesn't require more from us than we can do. In Matthew 10:42, we are taught that if a cup of water is all God has given you, then a cup of water is all that God requires. I know that today we don't go around offering strangers a cup of water as someone might in Bible times. However, today we have to respond to our opportunities that God presents to us. We ask co-workers to lunch, next time ask them to church. We tell our friends about that wonderful shoe sale, next time tell them what God means to you. All these are simple starts and are not big extravagant actions. When simple starts become part of your daily life, many thirsty people are found.

The second part of Step 1 is listening. How many people intend to follow God, but they haven't gotten around to it yet? They are too busy building their careers and their families and think that learning about God's plan is too hard. The Bible has many examples where people learned the plan of salvation and became Christians all in the same day. The Philippian jailer learned of the plan of salvation from Paul and Silas in Acts 16 and that same day he and his family were baptized. In this example, someone talked and someone listened — a whole family of somebodies!!

Paul and Silas looked for opportunities every day and sometimes opportunities just found them. Paul and Silas were successful, because they were ready to take advantage of their opportunities. They talked about their faith — sometimes people listened and sometimes people did not listen. The book of Acts has many inspiring stories to teach us of these successes and also has the stories where the people did not listen. For example, the Jews of Thessalonica hated the men who had turned the world upside down (Acts 17). Paul and Silas were talking and those Jews from Thessalonica were not listening. Instead, they gathered a mob and attacked the house of Jason where Paul and Silas had been staying. Wouldn't it have been wonderful if these people had reacted like the Philippian jailer? After hearing the gospel from Paul and Silas, the jailer and his household were baptized that night. The Philippian jailer not only heard Paul and Silas' preaching, but he was listening!

I agree that getting started is the hard part. You are only responsible for your part — the talking part. All of us must look for small opportunities to offer our cup of water and be ready for opportunities to be like Paul and Silas. All of us must be ready to start and talk to others about our faith and the plan of salvation. Some will listen and others will not, but we will have started!

The Freewill of Our Children

In Proverbs 22:6, Solomon taught, *"Train up a child in the way he should go, and when he is old he will not depart from it."* So if we have trained up our children to follow God and they don't follow God when they are grown, are we bad parents?

A proverb is a truthful saying from a wise person. This Proverb was written by Solomon who asked God for wisdom, so he definitely was a wise man. Today, more than ever, we need to teach our children with Biblical guidance and direction while they are young to establish a strong foundation for their future. Faithful children are so important that they are among the qualifications for elders in Titus and 1 Timothy.

As I am raising my children, I teach them the truth, bring them to church, and try to be a good example to them. Will they depart from the path? Let's see what else the Bible teaches us about raising children.

We will start with our wise man, Solomon. Early in his kingship, Solomon walked with God and even asked God for wisdom to rule his kingdom. God blessed Solomon and made him a rich man also. Solomon's son, Rehoboam, was king after Solomon's death (1 Kings 12:1-24). When the people came to Rehoboam to ask for lighter taxes, Rehoboam followed the counsel of his young friends and did not ask God. Of course, Rehoboam got the wrong answer from his young friends. Why did Rehoboam do that when he knew about God? He did that because God had given him the free will to choose to ask Him or not. Rehoboam chose to follow the counsel of the young men and did not choose to follow God.

Another kingly example is Hezekiah, son of Ahaz. Hezekiah was one of the great kings of the southern kingdom and did right in the sight of God (2 Kings 18:3-8). Hezekiah's father, Ahaz, worshiped idols, closed the temple, and sought help from Assyria instead of God (2 Kings 16). There is no way that Hezekiah learned about God from his father. Hezekiah purified the temple, restored temple worship and Passover celebrations, and destroyed his father's idols and altars. Hezekiah chose to follow God regardless of the lack of training from his father. Again God gave Hezekiah the free will to follow Him or to follow the horrible example of his father, King Ahaz.

There are Biblical examples of great Christians who had good training as a child from their parents. Timothy was taught by his mother and grandmother, Eunice and Lois (2 Timothy 1:5). Timothy was an early leader in the first century church and his faith is an example to us today. Timothy did not have to continue as he had been taught, because he had freewill to follow God or not. However, because Timothy had early teaching and then a strong personal conviction, he followed God.

God gave everyone freewill as he wanted His people to follow Him, because they wanted to – not because they had to follow. Adam and Eve are a good example. God walked with them in the cool of the evening, because He loved them and all of His creation. However, He allowed them to choose to obey Him with regard to eating from the Tree of the Knowledge of Good and Evil. This same choice is given to all of God's people including us AND our children.

As parents, we must give our children knowledge of God and be good examples for them. Proverbs 1:8 tells our young people to *"hear the instruction of your father and do not forsake the law of your mother."* It is clear in this verse that the wise writer understood the free will of grown children. I hope that I have taught my children well so that they will not depart from the path. However, whether I taught them well or not, the choice to follow God is theirs to make using the free will that God gave them.

Is Growing a Church Like Growing a Business?

Recently I was driving by one of the mega-churches in my city. This church clearly had a strong building program as it was adding a new building to its already large campus. The church members I know from this church are proud of their church's accomplishments and work hard on the church projects. This group is considered one of the most successful and influential churches in my city. Since I am also a business person, I wondered, "Is growing a church like growing a business?"

A successful business must know what its product is and what their customers want in that product. A successful business will market their product by making sure the customer knows how their product is better than a competing product. Differentiators are identified to show customers why the successful business is better at delivering the product to the customer. This business has their focus on the customer to ensure that the delivered product is the product desired by the customer. Many churches follow this business plan as they work hard to serve the community and their members. The church offers products and services to the community with a strong customer focus.

Churches that follow this business plan may be promoting a type of social gospel. These churches are doing good things for the community, but may be prioritizing social requirements over New Testament teaching with their focus on their customers instead of God.

The business of a church must be God-focused and so a business model for growing a church does not apply. Instead of differentiating the church's products for the customers, the focus of a successful church is on God. This focus does not necessarily consider how the church can help the community, but determines what spiritual work God wants the church to do in the community. The work of the church is described to us in the New Testament as evangelism, edification of Christians, and benevolence for saints.

The primary mission of a God-focused church is to spread and teach the gospel to those who are not Christians. Matthew 28:19-20 is often referred to as the Great Commission. *"Go therefore and make disciples of all the nations, baptizing them in the name of the Father and of the Son and of the Holy Spirit, teaching them to observe all things that I have commanded you."* Evangelism was alive in New Testament times. The book of Acts is full of examples of churches working to spread the gospel across their known world. Our churches must also work hard to evangelize within our communities and our known world!

Edification of the saints includes assembly, fellowship, encouragement to remain faithful, and inspiring each other with the truth. In Hebrews 10:24-25, the church is reminded that edification of the saints is an important work of the church. *"And let us consider one another in order to stir up love and good works, not forsaking the assembling of ourselves together, as is the manner of some, but exhorting one another, and so much the more as you see the Day approaching."* A church cannot be strong that is lacking spiritual edification among its members.

Benevolence is also an important work of a church. Care of the saints is most important, but Christians must also *"do good"* for non-Christians. This is very clear in Galatians 6:9-10. *"And let us not grow weary while doing good, for in due season we shall reap if we do not lose heart. Therefore, as we have opportunity, let us do good to all, especially to those who are of the household of faith."* Doing good works does not justify a Christian, but is a fruit of his Christianity and a result of the spiritual sowing of the Christian. A strong church considers benevolence as a central work.

A successful church must know what God wants the work of the church to be. The works desired by the members is secondary to God's requirements and so a church cannot be grown like a business with customer focus. Customer focus works for a business, but not a church. A church must focus on God — striving to do His work which is evangelism, edification of Christians, and benevolence for saints.

Practice and Study

Are you too busy for daily Bible study and prayer? Current statistics* tell us that 67.6% of Americans work more than forty hours per week. U.S. workers have no legislated minimum number of vacation days to be provided by their employers and they can certainly feel the work pressure. Children are overscheduled with school, sports, and other extracurricular activities. Our lives are busy, on the go, and demanding. No one has time for daily Bible study and prayer with our contemporary pressure-cooker lives. Or do we?

First let's agree that being a Christian is our goal. We can also have other goals, such as, to be an athlete, musician, doctor, or soldier. To be an athlete requires off season conditioning, pre-season practice, and both practice and game time during the sports season. A great athlete requires commitment and mental endurance to compete and to finish. To be a musician requires hours of training and practice before playing on any stage. To be a doctor requires years of education and then years of internship. Frequent tests, seminars and studies certify that a doctor maintains adequate competence in his area of expertise and are required throughout the doctor's career. Soldiers practice war craft every day and learn new skills to protect our country. Time, practice, study, and commitment are all necessary to be an athlete, musician, doctor, or soldier. Are time, practice, study, and commitment necessary to be a Christian?

Daniel customarily prayed in his upper room with his windows open three time a day (Daniel 6:10). He was also a governor reporting directly to King Darius, was an advisor to King Nebuchadnezzar and interpreted handwriting for King Belshazzar. Daniel was a busy man, but daily found time to pray and to be pleasing to God. Daniel was a successful leader in Babylon, but kept his duties to God as his first priority.

King David is another example of a busy man who made God his first priority. David ruled and expanded Israel, built political alliances, and led a great army. He took the shaky kingdom left to him by Saul and made Israel a dominant force. The psalms written by David as prayers and praises to God are evidence of the time, practice, study, and commitment that David made to God. The Bible tells us that King David was a man after God's own heart (1 Samuel 13:14) which proves that a busy man can make time for God.

The best example of a busy man who made private time with God is Jesus. Jesus traveled in Galilee, Samaria, and Judea preaching and teaching to all that would listen. He taught His disciples so that they could teach after He was not with them anymore. His teaching and miracles drew crowds of thousands which left little opportunity for private time with God. However, Jesus frequently withdrew from His disciples and the crowds to pray to God. For example, after feeding the 5000 men plus more women and children, Jesus went to the mountain by Himself to pray (Matthew 14:23). Probably the best known example of Jesus praying alone is in the Garden of Gethsemane before He was arrested by the Jews (Matthew 26:36-45). Jesus was committed to pleasing God as His first priority in His busy life.

We that have the goal to be a Christian must make the time to prepare ourselves. As the athlete prepares with off season conditioning, we must prepare by studying our Bible. As the musician and doctor practice their professions, we must daily put our Christian faith to work by applying our Bible lessons. As the soldier learns new skills before going to war, we must use our Bible to learn about God. Christianity takes time, practice, study, and commitment from us in the twenty-first century just as it was required from first century Christians. Make God your priority and you will find the time for daily prayer and study.

*quoted statistics are from *www.nationsmaster.com*

An Ahaa Moment

Most of us have had an "Ahaa Moment" when you understand something that you have always known. Recently my twenty-something son shared an Ahaa Moment that he had experienced. During a Bible study, the discussion was about God's promise to Abram for an heir from Abram's body. In Genesis 15:5 the verse says, *"Then He brought him outside and said, 'Look now toward heaven, and count the stars if you are able to number them.' And He said to him, 'So shall your descendants be.'"* My son knew Abram's story well and had read the verse many times. His Ahaa Moment was the understanding that those stars which Abram could see were the same stars that he could see each night. This understanding brought him a new appreciation of the power of God and grandeur of His creation. My son drew closer to God after experiencing this Moment and uses his Moment to tell others of his faith and the greatness of God. Often an Ahaa Moment spurs the person experiencing the Moment into action. Let's see if we can find examples in the New Testament of Ahaa Moments.

Paul was a passionate Jewish leader that defended his Jewish faith with persecution of early Jewish Christians. He believed in God and the Jewish law and made the early Christians pay with their lives for leaving the Jewish faith. Of course, we know the story of Paul's trip to Damascus where Jesus spoke to Paul on the road (Acts 9:1-20). Paul's Ahaa

Moment was when he understood that Jesus was Christ and the Son of God who was sent to earth for man's salvation which fulfilled Old Testament prophecy. After Ananias baptized Paul, Paul immediately began preaching about Christ in the synagogues. Paul used his Ahaa Moment to preach and teach others about Christianity and to become a teacher for Christians throughout the centuries.

The Ethiopian treasurer was *"of great authority under Candace the queen of the Ethiopians, who had charge of all her treasury, and had come to Jerusalem to worship"* (Acts 8:27). That the Ethiopian had traveled some fifteen hundred miles to worship demonstrates that he was a devout Jewish worshiper of God and that he was reading from the book of Isaiah demonstrates his knowledge of God. The Ethiopian's Ahaa Moment was when Philip preached Jesus to him (Acts 8:35) and the Ethiopian understood that Christ was the Son of God (Acts 8:37) as was prophesied in the book of Isaiah. Of course, his Ahaa Moment required action and the Ethiopian was immediately baptized (Acts 8:38).

A third wonderful example of an Ahaa Moment is the story of Cornelius. In Acts 10:2, we are told that Cornelius was *"a devout man and one who feared God with all his household, who gave alms generously to the people, and prayed to God always."* Cornelius had sent for Peter because of instructions from an angel in a vision. By the time Peter arrived, Cornelius had assembled his relatives and close friends (who were all Gentiles) to hear from Peter all the things commanded by God. Cornelius knew something great was going to happen and was prepared to share with all the people he loved! The Ahaa Moment of this story really happened to the Jewish Christians that came with Peter. These Christians knew Peter said God had shown him to not call any man common or unclean (Acts 10:28). While Peter was preaching to Cornelius and all the Gentiles that were gathered with him, the

Holy Spirit fell upon Cornelius and all those Gentiles (Acts 10:44-45). When Peter and the Jewish Christians saw that, they understood that salvation was for both Jew and Gentile and that was an Ahaa Moment for those Jewish Christians! Knowing what Peter said before and was preaching to Cornelius wasn't enough. They had to see the gift of the Holy Spirit on the Gentiles to understand that the gospel was for all. With this Ahaa Moment, Peter commanded the Gentiles to be baptized.

Ahaa Moments are a call to action. When your Moment clarifies your understanding of your faith in God, you can be like Paul, the Ethiopian, or the Jewish Christians. Sometimes your new understanding simply causes you to tell others of your faith with more strength and conviction or maybe your Ahaa Moment will be dramatic like the Christians of the first century. Every Ahaa Moment is a singular moment that can have a ripple effect that influences many people. Your effect can be like Paul's with influence that last centuries. How can you know? Let your Ahaa Moment be your call to action!

Storms and Preparedness

I lived in north Alabama during the tornado outbreak of April 27, 2011. Sixty one tornadoes touched down across Alabama with an F5 tornado very close to my home. I couldn't watch the news coverage about them due to the lack of electricity. The tornadoes had destroyed so much of the power grid that most people had no power for almost a week. I am told the pictures of devastation were emotional and overwhelming during the news coverage of this week. As I write these thoughts, 232 Alabamians have lost their lives in these storms and countless homes and business are destroyed.

My husband and I are prepared for tornado storms with a storm shelter that is accessible from inside our home. We had gathered my father with us for the day to watch for potential danger to us. As we watched the F5 tornado come close to our house, we hurried my father into the shelter. This tornado missed us, but hit so many of our friends' homes and destroyed my father's church building.

During the storm, we discovered we really were not very prepared. For example, we don't keep supplies in the shelter; we had to search for working flashlights; our candles and matches were not together; the radio was in the garage; and we had no fresh batteries for the flashlights and radio. We had gotten so comfortable watching weather news on our living room couch that we were not prepared for a real storm. Contemporary living had taught us that weather news happens to someone else — tsunamis happen to Japan, hurricanes happen to New Orleans, flooding happens to Missouri and Mississippi, and forest fires happen to Texas. You don't have to be prepared for a storm when storms happen to someone else.

Compare our storm preparedness to Jesus' parable of the ten virgins (Matthew 25:1-13). As part of the wedding custom of the time, the bridegroom went to the bride's house to get her and bring her back to his home. The wedding guests wait along the path to follow the groom with his bride back to his home for the wedding feast. They use lamps to light the way as there were no streetlamps in these ancient times. In this parable, five virgins brought extra oil for their lamps in case the groom was delayed. They were prepared and ready for the groom to come anytime. The five other virgins did not have extra oil and so ran out before the groom returned with his bride. While the five unprepared virgins went to buy more lamp oil, the groom came. Everyone went into the house for the feast and the doors were closed. These five unprepared virgins were turned away at the door and could not get into the feast. Their preparations were cursory as they had lamps without enough oil. They were not prepared when the groom came!

In this parable, the groom is Christ, all of us are the virgins, and heaven is the wedding feast. We know that the Groom is coming, but not when. We are invited to the wedding feast, but must be prepared with our lamps full of oil to light the way for the wedding party. If we are not prepared, we will be turned away as were the five unprepared virgins. Preparation for Christ's return is not the same as stocking up on fresh batteries. Daily study of our Bibles and prayer is the basic preparation. This preparation helps us to know what God wants us to do to be prepared for Christ's return!

Grudges and Forgiveness and Forgetting

Recently someone told me "holding a grudge is letting someone else use your mind for free." A grudge is resentment for some remembered wrong from a small slight to a great evil deed. Remembering a grudge causes us to focus on past sins against us instead of moving forward in our lives. The two main points to be made in a discussion about grudges are forgiveness and forgetting.

In Matthew 18: 21-35, Jesus tells a parable about these two points. In this parable, a servant owed the king ten thousand talents. In today's money, this is about two billion dollars – an impossible amount to repay! The king was going to sell the servant's family into slavery and take all the servant's possessions. The servant pleaded for forgiveness of the great debt and the compassionate king did just that. The servant no longer owed the king! Later a second servant owed the first servant a small amount of money. The first servant demanded full payment from the second servant had the second servant thrown into debtor's prison until the amount was repaid. Of course, the king hears about this controversy and reminds the first servant of his great debt that had been forgiven. He told the servant that the same compassion should be shown to the second servant. Because the first servant had not forgiven the small debt from the second servant, the king now demanded full payment of the great debt from the first servant!

Jesus frequently taught His disciples that we must forgive each other. Right before the above parable, he told Peter, "*I do not say to you, up to seven times, but up to seventy times seven*" meaning Peter should be willing to forgive a person every time he repented of having sinned against him. When He taught the desciples how to pray in Matthew 6:8-15, He included, "*And forgive us our debts as we forgive our debtors,*" and also said, "*for if you forgive men their trespasses, your heavenly Father will also forgive you. But if you do not forgive men their trespasses, neither will you father forgive your trespasses.*" Jesus expected us to forgive others of small slights to great evil deeds. He even asked the Father to forgive the people of His crucifixion before He died on the cross (Luke 23:34).

Sometimes I wonder if I have truly forgiven, if I have not forgotten. After all in Hebrews 8:12, God tells us, "*For I will be merciful to their unrighteousness, and their sins and their lawless deeds I will remember no more.*" If my goal is to be like God and God forgets my sins, shouldn't I also forget others' sins against me? I struggle with forgetting a sin against me. I just cannot dump the memory and not remember the sin.

Let's go back to the parable about the servant and the great debt. The main point of this parable is that we must forgive others, because God has already forgiven us of so much. However, the king had not forgotten the debt, but had put that memory into the dusty attic of his mind! He had forgiven the servant of the debt and was not going to collect the money owed to him until the first servant put the second servant into debtor's prison for a small amount of money.

The king collected the money from the first servant because of that servant's pattern of bad behavior, not because the first servant had not been forgiven.

God does not require the impossible from us. Forgiveness is required, but He knows we cannot selectively delete memories. He does require that we do not nurse those memories into grudges. If we truly forgive others of their sins against us, then we cannot dwell on those sins. We must act as if we had forgotten the sin as we forgive others of that sin! We must actively seek love and goodwill toward all who have sinned against us (Romans 12:20). Nobody ever said it wasn't hard to forgive and then forget.

What Did You Do Today?

Have you ever gotten to the end of the day and wondered what you had accomplished with your time? Everyone has the same amount of time in each day. We all have twenty-four hours in a day, sixty minutes in an hour, and sixty seconds in a minute – no more and no less. God may have given us different abilities and talents, but He gave us the same amount of time. So what did you do today with the time and abilities that God has given to you?

Jesus teaches His disciples in the parable of the talents (Matthew 25:14-29) about the use of our time and abilities. During New Testament times, a talent is a piece of money, not a skill or ability as we use the word today. In this parable, the master gives a different amount of talents (money) to three servants depending on their individual abilities. When the master comes back, he calls the three servants to him for an accounting of his money. The first two servants had worked hard making good use of their time and made a profit with the master's money. The last servant was fearful of risking the master's money and so hid his talents in a hole. The master was so mad and threw the servant in outer darkness! He had expected the servant to at least make an effort! This particular servant had received the same time and least money from the master, because he had the least ability of the three servants. However, the master still expected the less capable servant to use the abilities that he had to look for opportunities.

Today a lot of people are like the third servant, because they are not looking for opportunities to use their abilities. They wait on more capable people to make a difference in their communities and church families and with each missed opportunity is lost time. Neither the time nor opportunity can be rewound – they are gone. All of us have capabilities to work in God's kingdom performing valuable tasks and all of us, for sure, have the same amount of time. We just need to quit waiting on others, get up from our comfortable chairs, and make the effort.

There is an old adage, "If you want something done, ask a busy person." Strive to be a person who uses time well, not just a busy person. Busy-ness is not the goal, but working profitably for God. Make sure that the tasks that keep you busy are the most important tasks. When looking for opportunities to work for God, we often have to look at ourselves and then outward to others. Consider what things would make you happy and do those things for someone else. If a cold cup of water is all that we have, that is all that God demands (Mark 9:41).

Have you ever complained about the lack of support from your Christian brethren? Well turn that complaint back on yourself. What have you done for them? Simple gestures can make a big difference for others. In Acts, the early Christians went gladly from house to house fellowshipping with one another. When was the last time that you visited someone? Dropped in on the older couple? Visited a chronically ill child? Completed a chore for the widow? Not all opportunities require money. They require your time which is the most valuable talent that you have. I know these reminders seem trite, but not to our brethren who are having a hard time. Everyone likes to be remembered!

Once you have practiced with simple tasks, step out of your comfort zone. In lots of congregations, the work is often done by the same group of people all the time. Volunteer for a task that you have not performed before. You may learn a new skill that you really enjoy. Greet visitors and engage them in a meaningful conversation. Talk to church members who do not sit close to you. Really shake things up and sit in a different pew! Don't wait for other Christians to engage you as they are probably waiting too! Visiting at other congregations is encouraging to both you and others. Being a Christian example is noticeable in the workplace and our children's ballgames. The goal is not to blend in, but let your light shine!

Then we step up our game and look for bigger opportunities. Reach out to your neighbor to come to church with you. Write your thoughts in an article like this one (who knows whom you will reach then?). Actively looking for opportunities makes wonderful use of time and abilities. Our actions are like the pebble thrown into a still pond. The ripples get bigger and bigger and involve more and more of the pond when people demonstrate their Christian beliefs. If you teach one person about Christ, you are making ripples in the pond! You do not know where your influence will stop when you use your opportunities for good.

We cannot say that we are not capable of working in God's kingdom. That wasn't an effective defense for the third servant and isn't a defense for us. We have to consciously look for the opportunity and then persevere. God gave all of us many different abilities, but He gave us all the same amount of time. It is our responsibility to use both wisely. So, what did you do today?

Epilogue

First I would like to thank God for the opportunity to work on my articles in this book. He has blessed me in so many ways! Also I would like to thank everyone for reading my book. After working many years, I began my retirement with a goal of writing a book. If you have enjoyed it, I hope you will share it with your friends, neighbors, and coworkers. There is nothing better than a book that has been read and passed along.

I live in Madison, Alabama with my husband, Ray, and attend church at the Church of Christ on Gooch Lane in Madison. I really want to thank Ray for his encouragement. He has been wonderful as I work on my projects! We have two sons, Adam and Scott. Adam is serving in the Navy on the USS Hue City. Scott is studying at the University of Alabama in Birmingham. We are so proud of both of them.

For articles from other authors, I can recommend these websites, *www.teachingtruth.org* and *www.spreadingtruth. org*. I know that there are many more and regret not listing all of them.

Again, thank you for reading my book. It is my first book and I hope that it is not my last one!

www.ingramcontent.com/pod-product-compliance
Lightning Source LLC
Chambersburg PA
CBHW021210020426
42331CB00003B/290

* 9 7 8 1 5 8 4 2 7 3 4 0 0 *